My Microadventures

The diary for short local outdoor experiences (#6)

Leo Vollgeherzt

vollgeherzt

This book belongs to:

About me and my outdoor passion:

My equipment:

My microadventure

○   ○   ○   ○

Description

Date / period

Weather conditions   ○   ○   ○   ○   ○   ○

Start

Destination

Companions / experiences / particularities / details

Map

My microadventure

Description

Date / period

Weather conditions

Start

Destination

Companions / experiences / particularities / details

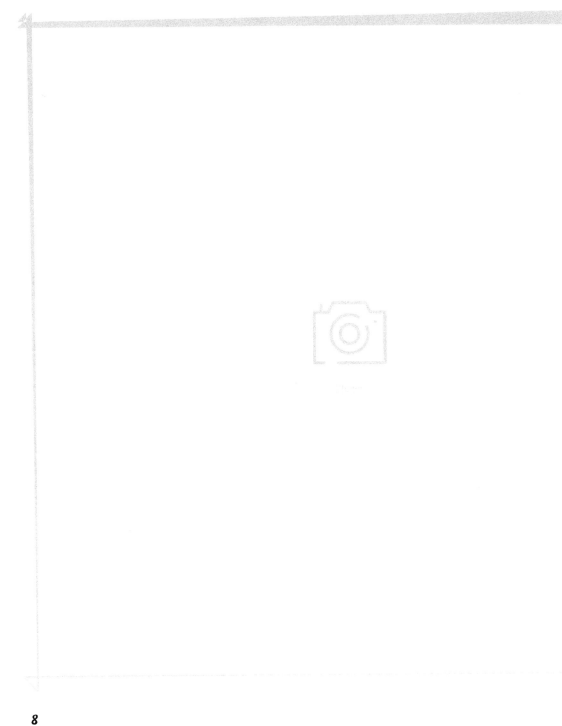

My microadventure

○   ○   ○   ○

Description

Date / period

Weather conditions   ○   ○   ○   ○   ○   ○

Start

Destination

Companions / experiences / particularities / details

My microadventure

○ 😍   ○ 🙂   ○ 😐   ○ ☹️

Description

Date / period

Weather conditions   ○ ☀️   ○ ⛅   ○ ☁️   ○ 🌧️   ○ ⚡   ○ ❄️

Start

Destination

Companions / experiences / particularities / details

My microadventure

○   ○   ○   ○

Description

Date / period

Weather conditions   ○   ○   ○   ○   ○   ○

Start

Destination

Companions / experiences / particularities / details

My microadventure

○ 😍   ○ 🙂   ○ 😐   ○ 😞

Description

Date / period

Weather conditions   ○ ☀️   ○ ⛅   ○ ☁️   ○ 🌧️   ○ ⚡   ○ ❄️

Start

Destination

Companions / experiences / particularities / details

My microadventure

○ 😍   ○ 🙂   ○ 😐   ○ ☹️

Description

Date / period

Weather conditions   ○ ☀️   ○ ⛅   ○ ☁️   ○ 🌧️   ○ ⚡   ○ ❄️

Start

Destination

Companions / experiences / particularities / details

My microadventure

○ 😍   ○ 🙂   ○ 😐   ○ ☹️

Description

Date / period

Weather conditions   ○ ☀️   ○ ⛅   ○ ☁️   ○ 🌧️   ○ ⚡   ○ ❄️

Start

Destination

Companions / experiences / particularities / details

My microadventure

○ 😍   ○ ☺   ○ 😐   ○ ☹

Description

Date / period

Weather conditions   ○ ☀   ○ ⛅   ○ ☁   ○ 🌧   ○ ⚡   ○ ❄

Start

Destination

Companions / experiences / particularities / details

My microadventure

○ 😍   ○ ☺   ○ 😐   ○ ☹

Description

Date / period

Weather conditions   ○ ☀   ○ ⛅   ○ ☁   ○ 🌧   ○ ⚡   ○ ❄

Start

Destination

Companions / experiences / particularities / details

My microadventure

○ 😍   ○ 🙂   ○ 😐   ○ ☹️

Description

Date / period

Weather conditions   ○ ☀️   ○ ⛅   ○ ☁️   ○ 🌧️   ○ ⚡   ○ ❄️

Start

Destination

Companions / experiences / particularities / details

My microadventure

○ 😍   ○ 🙂   ○ 😐   ○ ☹️

Description

Date / period

Weather conditions   ○ ☀️   ○ ⛅   ○ ☁️   ○ 🌧️   ○ ⚡   ○ ❄️

Start

Destination

Companions / experiences / particularities / details

My microadventure

○ 😍 ○ 🙂 ○ 😐 ○ ☹️

Description

Date / period

Weather conditions ○ ☀️   ○ ⛅   ○ ☁️   ○ 🌧️   ○ ⚡   ○ ❄️

Start

Destination

Companions / experiences / particularities / details

My microadventure ○ 😍   ○ 🙂   ○ 😐   ○ ☹️

Description

Date / period

Weather conditions   ○ ☀️   ○ ⛅   ○ ☁️   ○ 🌧️   ○ ⚡   ○ ❄️

Start

Destination

Companions / experiences / particularities / details

My microadventure

○ ○ ○  ○

Description

Date / period

Weather conditions   ○   ○   ○   ○   ○   ○

Start

Destination

Companions / experiences / particularities / details

My microadventure

○ 😍   ○ 🙂   ○ 😐   ○ ☹️

Description

Date / period

Weather conditions   ○ ☀️   ○ ⛅   ○ ☁️   ○ 🌧️   ○ ⚡   ○ ❄️

Start

Destination

Companions / experiences / particularities / details

My microadventure

○ 😍 ○ 🙂 ○ 😐 ○ ☹️

Description

Date / period

Weather conditions   ○ ☀️   ○ ⛅   ○ ☁️   ○ 🌧️   ○ ⚡   ○ ❄️

Start

Destination

Companions / experiences / particularities / details

My microadventure

○ 😍   ○ 🙂   ○ 😐   ○ ☹️

Description

Date / period

Weather conditions ○ ☀️   ○ ⛅   ○ ☁️   ○ 🌧️   ○ ⚡   ○ ❄️

Start

Destination

Companions / experiences / particularities / details

My microadventure

○   ○   ○  ○

Description

Date / period

Weather conditions ○   ○   ○   ○   ○   ○

Start

Destination

Companions / experiences / particularities / details

My microadventure

○ 😍   ○ 🙂   ○ 😐   ○ ☹️

Description

Date / period

Weather conditions   ○ ☀️   ○ ⛅   ○ ☁️   ○ 🌧️   ○ ⚡   ○ ❄️

Start

Destination

Companions / experiences / particularities / details

My microadventure

○   ○   ○   ○

Description

Date / period

Weather conditions   ○   ○   ○   ○   ○   ○

Start

Destination

Companions / experiences / particularities / details

My microadventure

○ 😍   ○ 🙂   ○ 😐   ○ ☹️

Description

Date / period

Weather conditions   ○ ☀️   ○ ⛅   ○ ☁️   ○ 🌧️   ○ ⚡   ○ ❄️

Start

Destination

Companions / experiences / particularities / details

My microadventure

○ 😍   ○ 🙂   ○ 😐   ○ ☹️

Description

Date / period

Weather conditions   ○ ☀️   ○ ⛅   ○ ☁️   ○ 🌧️   ○ ⚡   ○ ❄️

Start

Destination

Companions / experiences / particularities / details

My microadventure

○ 😍   ○ 🙂   ○ 😐   ○ ☹️

Description

Date / period

Weather conditions   ○ ☀️   ○ ⛅   ○ ☁️   ○ 🌧️   ○ ⚡   ○ ❄️

Start

Destination

Companions / experiences / particularities / details

My microadventure

○ 😍   ○ 🙂   ○ 😐   ○ ☹️

Description

Date / period

Weather conditions   ○ ☀️   ○ ⛅   ○ ☁️   ○ 🌧️   ○ ⚡   ○ ❄️

Start

Destination

Companions / experiences / particularities / details

My microadventure

○ 😍   ○ 🙂   ○ 😐   ○ ☹️

Description

Date / period

Weather conditions   ○ ☀️   ○ ⛅   ○ ☁️   ○ 🌧️   ○ ⚡   ○ ❄️

Start

Destination

Companions / experiences / particularities / details

My microadventure

○ 😍   ○ 🙂   ○ 😐   ○ ☹️

Description

Date / period

Weather conditions   ○ ☀️   ○ ⛅   ○ ☁️   ○ 🌧️   ○ ⚡   ○ ❄️

Start

Destination

Companions / experiences / particularities / details

My microadventure

○ 😍 ○ 🙂 ○ 😐 ○ ☹️

Description

Date / period

Weather conditions ○ ☀️   ○ ⛅   ○ ☁️   ○ 🌧️   ○ ⚡   ○ ❄️

Start

Destination

Companions / experiences / particularities / details

My microadventure

○   ○   ○   ○

Description

Date / period

Weather conditions   ○   ○   ○   ○   ○   ○

Start

Destination

Companions / experiences / particularities / details

My microadventure

○ 😍   ○ 🙂   ○ 😐   ○ ☹️

Description

Date / period

Weather conditions   ○ ☀️   ○ ⛅   ○ ☁️   ○ 🌧️   ○ ⚡   ○ ❄️

Start

Destination

Companions / experiences / particularities / details

My microadventure

○ 😍   ○ 🙂   ○ 😐   ○ ☹️

Description

Date / period

Weather conditions   ○ ☀️   ○ ⛅   ○ ☁️   ○ 🌧️   ○ ⚡   ○ ❄️

Start

Destination

Companions / experiences / particularities / details

My microadventure

○ 😍 ○ 🙂 ○ 😐 ○ ☹️

Description

Date / period

Weather conditions ○ ☀️ ○ ⛅ ○ ☁️ ○ 🌧️ ○ ⚡ ○ ❄️

Start

Destination

Companions / experiences / particularities / details

My microadventure

○ 😍   ○ 🙂   ○ 😐   ○ ☹️

Description

Date / period

Weather conditions   ○ ☀️   ○ ⛅   ○ ☁️   ○ 🌧️   ○ ⚡   ○ ❄️

Start

Destination

Companions / experiences / particularities / details

My microadventure

○ 😍　○ 🙂　○ 😐　○ ☹️

Description

Date / period

Weather conditions　　○ ☀️　　○ ⛅　　○ ☁️　　○ 🌧️　　○ ⚡　　○ ❄️

Start

Destination

Companions / experiences / particularities / details

My microadventure

○ 　○ 　○ 　○

Description

Date / period

Weather conditions　　○ 　　○ 　　○ 　　○ 　　○ 　　○

Start

Destination

Companions / experiences / particularities / details

My microadventure

○ 😍   ○ 🙂   ○ 😐   ○ ☹️

Description

Date / period

Weather conditions   ○ ☀️   ○ ⛅   ○ ☁️   ○ 🌧️   ○ ⚡   ○ ❄️

Start

Destination

Companions / experiences / particularities / details

My microadventure

○ 😍   ○ 🙂   ○ 😐   ○ ☹️

Description

Date / period

Weather conditions   ○ ☀️   ○ ⛅   ○ ☁️   ○ 🌧️   ○ ⚡   ○ ❄️

Start

Destination

Companions / experiences / particularities / details

My microadventure

○ 😍   ○ 🙂   ○ 😐   ○ ☹️

Description

Date / period

Weather conditions   ○ ☀️   ○ ⛅   ○ ☁️   ○ 🌧️   ○ ⚡   ○ ❄️

Start

Destination

Companions / experiences / particularities / details

My microadventure

○ ○ ○  ○

Description

Date / period

Weather conditions ○ ○ ○ ○ ○ ○

Start

Destination

Companions / experiences / particularities / details

My microadventure

○ 😍 ○ 🙂 ○ 😐 ○ ☹️

Description

Date / period

Weather conditions ○ ☀️ ○ ⛅ ○ ☁️ ○ 🌧️ ○ ⚡ ○ ❄️

Start

Destination

Companions / experiences / particularities / details

My microadventure

○ 😍   ○ 🙂   ○ 😐   ○ ☹️

Description

Date / period

Weather conditions   ○ ☀️   ○ ⛅   ○ ☁️   ○ 🌧️   ○ ⚡   ○ ❄️

Start

Destination

Companions / experiences / particularities / details

My microadventure

○   ○   ○   ○

Description

Date / period

Weather conditions   ○   ○   ○   ○   ○   ○

Start

Destination

Companions / experiences / particularities / details

My microadventure

○ 😍 ○ 🙂 ○ 😐 ○ ☹️

Description

Date / period

Weather conditions   ○ ☀️   ○ ⛅   ○ ☁️   ○ 🌧️   ○ ⚡   ○ ❄️

Start

Destination

Companions / experiences / particularities / details

My microadventure

○ 😍   ○ 🙂   ○ 😐   ○ ☹️

Description

Date / period

Weather conditions   ○ ☀️   ○ ⛅   ○ ☁️   ○ 🌧️   ○ ⚡   ○ ❄️

Start

Destination

Companions / experiences / particularities / details

My microadventure

○ 😍   ○ 🙂   ○ 😐   ○ ☹️

Description

Date / period

Weather conditions ○ ☀️   ○ ⛅   ○ ☁️   ○ 🌧️   ○ ⚡   ○ ❄️

Start

Destination

Companions / experiences / particularities / details

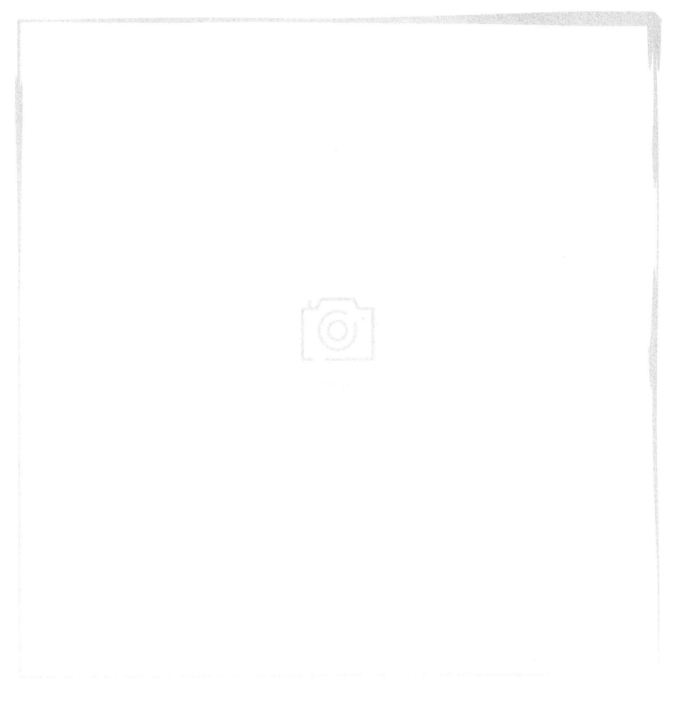

My microadventure

○  ○ ○ ○

Description

Date / period

Weather conditions ○   ○   ○   ○   ○   ○

Start

Destination

Companions / experiences / particularities / details

My microadventure

○   ○   ○   ○ ☹

Description

Date / period

Weather conditions ○   ○   ○   ○   ○   ○

Start

Destination

Companions / experiences / particularities / details

My microadventure

○ 😍   ○ 🙂   ○ 😐   ○ ☹️

Description

Date / period

Weather conditions   ○ ☀️   ○ ⛅   ○ ☁️   ○ 🌧️   ○ ⚡   ○ ❄️

Start

Destination

Companions / experiences / particularities / details

My microadventure

○ 😍   ○ 🙂   ○ 😐   ○ ☹️

Description

Date / period

Weather conditions   ○ ☀️   ○ ⛅   ○ ☁️   ○ 🌧️   ○ ⚡   ○ ❄️

Start

Destination

Companions / experiences / particularities / details

My microadventure

○ 😍   ○ 🙂   ○ 😐   ○ ☹️

Description

Date / period

Weather conditions   ○ ☀️   ○ ⛅   ○ ☁️   ○ 🌧️   ○ ⚡   ○ ❄️

Start

Destination

Companions / experiences / particularities / details

My microadventure

○ 😍 ○ 🙂 ○ 😐 ○ ☹️

Description

Date / period

Weather conditions   ○ ☀️   ○ ⛅   ○ ☁️   ○ 🌧️   ○ ⚡   ○ ❄️

Start

Destination

Companions / experiences / particularities / details

My microadventure

○ 😍   ○ 🙂   ○ 😐   ○ ☹️

Description

Date / period

Weather conditions   ○ ☀️   ○ ⛅   ○ ☁️   ○ 🌧️   ○ ⚡   ○ ❄️

Start

Destination

Companions / experiences / particularities / details

Imprint

© 2019 youneo projects flick und weber GbR

All rights reserved. The use of this book and any information contained in it is at one's own risk. Liability claims against the publisher and the author concerning either material or intellectual damage which is caused by the use or disuse of the presented information or through the use of faulty and/or incomplete information are fundamentally excluded. This work including all contents has been meticulously compiled. However, the publisher and the author do neither assume any liability for the timeliness, correctness, completeness and quality of the information displayed nor for any possible misprints.

Responsible

Christian Flick / Mathias Weber

youneo projects flick und weber GbR, Poststraße 1, 49326 Melle, Germany

kontakt@vollgeherzt.de, www.youneoprojects.de

Image sources

© Wantanee Chantasilp/shutterstock (Cover), © iHonn/shutterstock

vollgeherzt® is a registered trademark of youneo projects flick and weber GbR.

ISBN: 9781798717189

Made in the USA
Las Vegas, NV
22 December 2024